FOOTPRINTS
and
Other Inspirational Poems & Prayers

FOOTPRINTS

and

Other Inspirational Poems and Prayers

Edited by Jill Wolf

ISBN 0-89954-442-8

CONTENTS

ALL THINGS BRIGHT
AND BEAUTIFUL

All things bright and beautiful,
All creatures great and small,
All things wise and wonderful,
The Lord God made them all.

Each little flower that opens,
Each little bird that sings,
He made their glowing colours,
He made their tiny wings.

The purple-headed mountain,
The river running by,
The sunset, and the morning
That brightens up the sky,

The cold wind in the winter,
The pleasant summer sun,
The ripe fruits in the garden,
He made them every one.

The tall trees in the greenwood,
The meadows where we play,
The rushes by the water,
We gather every day.

He gave us eyes to see them,
And lips that we might tell
How great is God Almighty,
Who has made all things well.

—*Cecil Frances Alexander*

THE THINGS I PRIZE

These are the things I prize
And hold of dearest worth:
Light of the sapphire skies,
Peace of the silent hills,
Shelter of the forests,
    comfort of the grass,
Music of birds, murmur of little rills,
Shadows of cloud that swiftly pass,
And, after showers,
The smell of flowers
And of the good brown earth—
And best of all, along the way,
    friendship and mirth.

—Henry van Dyke

MATINS

Flowers rejoice when night is done,
Lift their heads to greet the sun;
Sweetest looks and odours raise,
In a silent hymn of praise.
So my heart would turn away
From the darkness to the day;
Lying open in God's sight
Like a flower in the light.

—Henry van Dyke

LIFE'S SWEETEST JOYS

Life's sweetest joys are hidden
In unsubstantial things;
An April rain, a fragrance,
A vision of blue wings...

—May Riley Smith

COUNT YOUR GARDEN

Count your garden by the flowers,
Never by the leaves that fall;
Count your days by golden hours,
Don't remember clouds at all.
Count your nights by stars, not shadows,
Count your years with smiles, not tears,
Count your blessings, not your troubles,
Count your age by friends, not years.

—Author Unknown

WHEN THE HEART
IS FULL OF LOVE

There is beauty in the forest
When the trees are green and fair,
There is beauty in the meadow
When wild flowers scent the air.
There is beauty in the sunlight
And the soft blue beams above.
Oh, the world is full of beauty
When the heart is full of love.

—Author Unknown

MAKING LIFE WORTHWHILE

Every soul that touches yours—
Be it the slightest contact—
Gets therefrom some good;
Some little grace; one kindly thought;
One aspiration yet unfelt;
One bit of courage
For the darkening sky;
One gleam of faith
To brave the thickening ills of life;
One glimpse of brighter skies—
To make this life worthwhile
And heaven a surer heritage.

—George Eliot

LEND A HAND

I am only one,
But still I am one.
I cannot do everything,
But still I can do something;
And because I cannot do everything
I will not refuse to do the something
that I can do.

—Edward Everett Hale

IF I CAN STOP ONE HEART FROM BREAKING

If I can stop one heart from breaking,
I shall not live in vain;
If I can ease one life the aching,
Or cool one pain,
Or help one fainting robin
Unto his nest again,
I shall not live in vain.

—Emily Dickinson

COUNT THAT DAY LOST

If you sit down at set of sun
And count the acts that you have done,
And, counting find
One self-denying deed, one word
That eased the heart of him who heard;
One glance most kind,
That fell like sunshine where it went—
Then you may count that day well spent.

But if, through all the livelong day,
You've cheered no heart, by yea or nay—
If, through it all
You've nothing done that you can trace
That brought the sunshine to one face—
No act most small
That helped some soul and nothing cost—
Then count that day as worse than lost.

—George Eliot

THE SWEETEST LIVES

The sweetest lives are those to duty wed,
Whose deeds, both great and small,
Are close-knit strands of unbroken thread
Where love ennobles all.
The world may sound no trumpets,
    ring no bells;
The book of life the shining record tells.

The love shall chant its own beatitudes
After its own life working. A child's kiss
Set on thy sighing lips shall make thee
    glad;
A sick man helped by thee shall make thee
    strong;
Thou shalt be served thyself by every sense
Of service which thou renderest.

—Attributed to Elizabeth Barrett Browning

MY TASK

To be honest, to be kind;
To earn a little and to spend a little less;
To make upon the whole a family happier
    for his presence;
To renounce when that shall be necessary
    and not to be embittered;
To keep a few friends, but those
    without capitulation;
Above all, on the same grim conditions,
    to keep friends with himself—
Here is a task for all that man has of
    fortitude and delicacy.

                      —Robert Louis Stevenson

THINGS THAT NEVER DIE

The pure, the bright, the beautiful
That stirred our hearts in youth,
The impulses to wordless prayer,
The streams of love and truth,
The longing after something lost,
The spirit's yearning cry,
The striving after better hopes—
These things can never die.

The timid hand stretched forth to aid
A brother in his need;
A kindly word in grief's dark hour
That proves a friend indeed;
The plea for mercy softly breathed,
When justice threatens high,
The sorrow of a contrite heart—
These things shall never die.

Let nothing pass, for every hand
Must find some work to do,
Lose not a chance to waken love—
Be firm and just and true.
So shall a light that cannot fade
Beam on thee from on high,
And angel voices say to thee—
"These things shall never die."

—*Charles Dickens*

THE WAY

Who seeks for heaven alone to save
    his soul,
May keep the path, but will not reach
    the goal;
While he who walks in love may
    wander far,
But God will bring him where the
    Blessed are.

—Henry van Dyke

I NEVER KNEW A NIGHT SO BLACK

I never knew a night so black
Light failed to follow on its track.
I never knew a storm so gray
It failed to have its clearing day.
I never knew such bleak despair
That there was not a rift, somewhere.
I never knew an hour so drear
Love could not fill it full of cheer!

—John Kendrick Bangs

THE LOVE OF A FRIEND

Friendship—
Like music heard on the waters,
Like pines when the wind passeth by,
Like pearls in the depths of the ocean,
Like stars that enamel the sky,
Like June and the odor of roses,
Like dew and the freshness of morn,
Like sunshine that kisseth the clover,
Like tassels of silk on the corn,
Like mountains that arch the blue heavens,
Like clouds when the sun dippeth low,
Like songs of birds in the forests,
Like brooks where the sweet waters flow,
Like dreams of Arcadian pleasures,
Like colors that gratefully blend,
Like everything breathing of kindness—
Like these is the love of a friend.

—A. P. Stanley

HUGS

There's something in a simple hug
That always warms the heart;
It welcomes us back home
And makes it easier to part.

A hug's a way to share the joy
And sad times we go through,
Or just a way for friends to say
They like you 'cause you're you.

Hugs are meant for anyone
For whom we really care,
From your grandma to your neighbor—
Or a cuddly teddy bear.

A hug is an amazing thing—
It's just the perfect way
To show the love we're feeling
But can't find the words to say.

It's funny how a little hug
Makes everyone feel good;
In every place and language,
It's always understood.

And hugs don't need equipment,
Special batteries or parts—
Just open up your arms
And open up your hearts.

—*Jill Wolf*

HOME IS WHERE THERE'S
ONE TO LOVE US

Home's not merely four square walls,
Though with pictures hung and gilded;
Home is where Affection calls,
Filled with shrines the Heart hath builded!
Home!—go watch the faithful dove,
Sailing 'neath the heaven above us;
Home is where there's one to love!
Home is where there's one to love us!

Home's not merely roof and room—
It needs something to endear it;
Home is where the heart can bloom,
Where there's some kind lip to cheer it!
What is home with none to meet,
None to welcome, none to greet us?
Home is sweet—and only sweet—
Where there's one we love to meet us!

—Charles Swain

HOME

The home we first knew
    on this beautiful earth,
The friends of our childhood,
    the place of our birth,
In the heart's inner chamber
    sung always will be,
As the shell ever sings of
    its home in the sea!
            —Frances Dana Gage

HOME, SWEET HOME

'Mid pleasures and palaces
    though we may roam,
Be it ever so humble,
    there's no place like home;
A charm from the sky
    seems to hallow us there,
Which, seek through the world,
    is ne'er met with elsewhere.
Home, home, sweet, sweet home!
There's no place like home,
    there's no place like home!
            —John Howard Payne

MOTHER

The spirit of home is Mother.
The charm of her love is there.
One knows the joy of her presence
And her ever tender care.

Friendships will sometimes vary,
The old are changed for the new.
But always the same dear Mother
Will gladden a lifetime through!

—Author Unknown

FATHER

The greatest gift I ever had,
Came from God—
I call him DAD.

—Author Unknown

23

CHILDREN LEARN WHAT THEY LIVE

If a child lives with criticism,
    he learns to condemn.
If a child lives with hostility,
    he learns to fight.
If a child lives with ridicule,
    he learns to be shy.
If a child lives with shame,
    he learns to feel guilty.
If a child lives with tolerance,
    he learns to be patient.
If a child lives with encouragement,
    he learns confidence.
If a child lives with praise,
    he learns to appreciate.
If a child lives with fairness,
    he learns justice.
If a child lives with security,
    he learns to have faith.
If a child lives with approval,
    he learns to like himself.
If a child lives with acceptance
    and friendship, he learns
    to find love in the world.

—Author Unknown

TEEN CREED

Don't let your parents down;
  they brought you up.
Be humble enough to obey;
  you may give orders someday.
Choose companions with care;
  you become what they are.
Guard your thoughts;
  what you think, you are.
Choose only a date
  who would make a good mate.
Be master of your habits,
  or they will master you.
Don't be a show-off when you drive;
  drive with safety and arrive.
Don't let the crowd pressure you;
  stand for something or you'll
  fall for anything.

—Author Unknown

APRIL RAIN

It is not raining rain to me,
It's raining daffodils;
In every dimpled drop I see
Wild flowers on the hills.

The clouds of gray engulf the day
And overwhelm the town;
It is not raining rain to me,
It's raining roses down.

It is not raining rain to me,
But fields of clover bloom,
Where any buccaneering bee
May find a bed and room.

A health unto the happy!
A fig for him who frets!—
It is not raining rain to me,
It's raining violets.

—Robert Loveman

TALK HAPPINESS

Talk happiness. The world is sad enough
Without your woe. No path is
    wholly rough.
Look for the places that are smooth
    and clear,
And speak of them to rest the weary ear
Of earth, so hurt by one continuous strain
Of mortal discontent and grief and pain.

Talk faith. The world is better off without
Your uttered ignorance and morbid doubt.
If you have faith in God, or man, or self,
Say so; if not, push back upon the shelf
Of silence all your thoughts till faith
    shall come,
No one will grieve because your lips
    are dumb.

Talk health. The dreary, never-ending tale
Of mortal maladies is worn and stale;
You cannot charm or interest or please
By harping on that minor chord, disease.
Say you are well, or all is well with you,
And God shall hear your words and
    make them true!

—Ella Wheeler Wilcox

WINGS

Be like the bird
That, pausing in her flight
Awhile on boughs too slight,
Feels them give way
Beneath her and yet sings,
Knowing that she hath wings.

—Victor Hugo

I NEVER SAW A MOOR

I never saw a moor,
I never saw the sea;
Yet know I how the heather looks,
And what a wave must be.
I never spoke with God,
Nor visited in heaven;
Yet certain am I of the spot
As if the chart were given.

—Emily Dickinson

FAITH AND SIGHT

So I go on, not knowing,
—I would not, if I might—
I would rather walk in the dark with God
Than go alone in the light;
I would rather walk with Him by faith
Than walk alone by sight.

—Mary Gardiner Brainard

THE ETERNAL GOODNESS

I know not where His islands lift
Their fronded palms in air;
I only know I cannot drift
Beyond His love and care.

—John Greenleaf Whittier

UNBELIEF

There is no unbelief;
Whoever plants a seed beneath the sod
And waits to see it push away the clod,
He trusts in God.

—Elizabeth York Case

FOOTPRINTS

One night a man had a dream. He dreamed he was walking along the beach with the Lord. Across the sky flashed scenes from his life. For each scene, he noticed two sets of footprints in the sand: one belonging to him, and the other to the Lord.

When the last scene of his life flashed before him, he looked back at the footprints in the sand. He noticed that many times along the path of his life there was only one set of footprints. He also noticed that it happened at the very lowest and saddest times in his life. This really bothered him and he questioned the Lord about it.

"Lord, You said that once I decided to follow You, You'd walk with me all the way. But I have noticed that during the most troublesome times in my life, there is only one set of footprints. I don't understand why when I needed You most You would leave me."

The Lord replied, "My son, My precious child, I love you and would never leave you. During your times of trial and suffering, when you see only one set of footprints, it was then that I carried you."

—*Author Unknown*

PEACE

With eager heart and will on fire,
I strove to win my great desire.
"Peace shall be mine," I said; but life
Grew bitter in the barren strife.

My soul was weary, and my pride
Was wounded deep; to Heaven I cried,
"God grant me peace or I must die";
The dumb stars glittered no reply.

Broken at last, I bowed my head,
Forgetting all myself, and said,
"Whatever comes, His will be done";
And in that moment peace was won.

—Henry van Dyke

HOPE

Hope, like a gleaming taper's light,
Adorns and cheers our way;
And still, as darker grows the night,
Emits a brighter ray.

—Oliver Goldsmith

HOPE IS THE THING
WITH FEATHERS

Hope is the thing with feathers
That perches in the soul,
And sings the tune without the words,
And never stops at all,

And sweetest in the gale is heard;
And sore must be the storm
That could abash the little bird
That kept so many warm.

I've heard it in the chillest land,
And on the strangest sea;
Yet, never, in extremity,
It asked a crumb of me.

—Emily Dickinson

LIFE

Life, believe, is not a dream
So dark as sages say;
Oft a little morning rain
Foretells a pleasant day.
                    —*Charlotte Brontë*

DEAF AND DUMB

Only the prism's obstruction shows aright
The secret of a sunbeam, breaks its light
Into the jewelled bow from blankest white;
So may a glory from defeat arise...
                    —*Robert Browning*

BEGIN AGAIN

Every day is a fresh beginning,
Every morn is the world made new.
You who are weary of sorrow and sinning,
Here is a beautiful hope for you,—
A hope for me and a hope for you.

Every day is a fresh beginning;
Listen, my soul, to the glad refrain,
And, spite of old sorrow and older sinning,
And puzzles forecasted and possible pain,
Take heart with the day, and begin again.

—Susan Coolidge

DON'T QUIT

Don't quit when the tide is lowest,
For it's just about to turn;
Don't quit over doubts and questions,
For there's something you may learn.

Don't quit when the night is darkest,
For it's just a while 'til dawn;
Don't quit when you've run the farthest,
For the race is almost won.

Don't quit when the hill is steepest,
For your goal is almost nigh;
Don't quit, for you're not a failure
Until you fail to try.

—Jill Wolf

A WINNER'S CREED

If you think you are beaten, you are;
If you think you dare not, you don't;
If you'd like to win, but think you can't,
It's almost a cinch you won't.

If you think you'll lose, you're lost,
For out in the world we find
Success begins with a person's faith;
It's all in the state of mind.

Life's battles don't always go
To the stronger or faster hand;
They go to the one who trusts in God
And always thinks "I can."

—Author Unknown

THE BUTTERFLY

I hold you at last in my hand,
Exquisite child of the air.
Can I ever understand
How you grew to be so fair?

You came to my linden tree
To taste its delicious sweet,
I sitting here in the shadow and shine
Playing around its feet.

Now I hold you fast in my hand,
You marvelous butterfly,
Till you help me to understand
The eternal mystery.

From that creeping thing in the dust
To this shining bliss in the blue!
God give me courage to trust
I can break my chrysalis too!

—Alice Freeman Palmer

NO STAR IS EVER LOST

Have we not all, amid life's petty strife,
Some pure ideal of a noble life
That once seemed possible?
Did we not hear
The flutter of its wings and feel it near,
And just within our reach? It was. And yet
We lost it in this daily jar and fret.
But still our place is kept and it will wait,
Ready for us to fill it, soon or late.
No star is ever lost we once have seen:
We always may be what we might
    have been.

—Adelaide A. Proctor

TAKE TIME

Take time to think;
    it is the source of power.
Take time to read;
    it is the foundation of wisdom.

Take time to play;
    it is the secret of staying young.
Take time to be quiet;
    it is the opportunity to seek God.

Take time to be aware;
    it is the opportunity to help others.
Take time to love and be loved;
    it is God's greatest gift.

Take time to laugh;
    it is the music of the soul.
Take time to be friendly;
    it is the road to happiness.

Take time to dream;
    it is what the future is made of.
Take time to pray;
    it is the greatest power on earth.

—Author Unknown

LIFE

Let me but live my life from year to year,
With forward face and unreluctant soul;
Not hurrying to, nor turning from, the goal;
Not mourning for the things that disappear
In the dim past, nor holding back in fear
From what the future veils;
    but with a whole
And happy heart, that pays its toll
To Youth and Age,
    and travels on with cheer.

So let the way wind up the hill or down,
O'er rough or smooth,
    the journey will be joy:
Still seeking what I sought when but a boy,
New friendship, high adventure,
    and a crown,
My heart will keep the courage
    of the quest,
And hope the road's last turn will
    be the best.

—Henry van Dyke

THE LORD'S PRAYER

Our Father in heaven,
　　hallowed be Your name,
　　Your kingdom come,
　　Your will be done
　　on earth as it is in heaven.
Give us today our daily bread.
Forgive us our debts,
　　as we also have forgiven our debtors.
And lead us not into temptation,
　　but deliver us from the evil one.

Matthew 6:9-13 (NIV)

EVENING PRAYER

Now I lay me down to sleep,
I pray the Lord my soul to keep;
If I should die before I wake,
I pray the Lord my soul to take.

—Author Unknown

THE PRAYER OF ST. FRANCIS

Lord, make me a channel of Thy peace
That where there is hatred I may bring love,
That where there is wrong I may bring
    the spirit of forgiveness,
That where there is discord I may bring
    harmony,
That where there is error I may bring truth,
That where there is doubt I may bring faith,
That where there is despair I may bring
    hope,
That where there are shadows I may bring
    Thy light,
That where there is sadness I may bring joy.

Lord, grant that I may seek rather
To comfort—than to be comforted;
To understand—than to be understood;
To love—than to be loved;
For it is by giving that one receives;
It is by self-forgetting that one finds;
It is by forgiving that one is forgiven;
It is by dying that one awakens to
    eternal life.

—St. Francis of Assisi

THE SERENITY PRAYER

O, God, grant us the serenity to accept
What cannot be changed;
The courage to change what can be
    changed;
And wisdom to know one from the other.
                    —*Reinhold Niebuhr*

A PRAYER FOR PEACE

Please shelter us, Lord, from the tempest,
When the storm of war starts to break;
Please quiet our fear and our anger
As You calmed the great storm on the lake.

Allow us to harbor forgiveness,
When the crisis is finally past;
Let us build a bridge like a rainbow
To bring peace between people at last.

If we could have only one prayer, Lord,
That You answered in whole or in part,
Let our longing for peace be
    that prayer, Lord—
A prayer that's in everyone's heart.
                    —*Jill Wolf*

JUST FOR TODAY, LORD

I will live through the next twelve hours and not try to tackle all of life's problems at once. I will improve my mind. I will learn something useful. I will learn something that requires effort, thought, and concentration.

I will be agreeable. I will look my best, speak in a well-modulated voice, be courteous and considerate. I will not find fault with friend, relative, or colleague. I will not try to change or improve anyone but myself.

I will have a program. I might not follow it exactly, but I will have it. I will save myself from two enemies—hurry and indecision.

I will do a good turn and keep it a secret. If anyone finds out, it won't count. I will do two things I don't want to do, just for the exercise.

I will believe in myself. I will give my best to the world and feel confident that the world will give its best to me.

—Author Unknown

MORNING PRAYER

The day returns and brings us the petty
round of irritating concerns and duties.
Help us to play the man, help us to perform
them with laughter and kind faces, let
cheerfulness abound with industry.
Give us to go blithely on our business all
this day, bring us to our resting beds weary
and content and undishonored, and grant us
in the end the gift of sleep.

—Robert Louis Stevenson

OUR PRAYER

Thou hast given so much to me,
Give one thing more—a grateful heart;
Not thankful when it pleaseth me,
As if Thy blessings had spare days;
But such a heart, whose pulse may
    be Thy praise.

—George Herbert

Prayer for Family Blessing

Lord, behold our family here assembled.
We thank Thee for this place in which we
dwell; for the love that unites us; for the
peace accorded us this day; for the hope
with which we expect the morrow; for the
health, the work, the food, and the bright
skies, that make our lives delightful; for
our friends in all parts of the earth, and our
friendly helpers in this foreign isle. Let
peace abound in our small company. Purge
out of every heart the lurking grudge. Give
us grace and strength to forbear and to
persevere. Offenders, give us the grace to
accept and to forgive offenders. Forgetful
ourselves, help us to bear cheerfully the
forgetfulness of others. Give us courage
and gaiety and the quiet mind. Spare to us
our friends, soften to us our enemies.
Bless us, if it may be, in all our innocent
endeavours. If it may not, give us the
strength to encounter that which is to come,
that we may be brave in peril, constant in
tribulation, temperate in wrath, and in all
changes of fortune down to the gates
of death, loyal and loving one to another.

—Robert Louis Stevenson

THE POET'S PRAYER

If there be some weaker one,
Give me strength to help him on;
If a blinder soul there be,
Let me guide him nearer Thee;
Make my mortal dreams come true
With the work I fain would do;
Clothe with life the weak intent,
Let me be the thing I meant;
Let me find in Thy employ,
Peace that dearer is than joy;
Out of self to love be led,
And to heaven acclimated,
Until all things sweet and good
Seem my natural habitude.

— John Greenleaf Whittier

A BLESSING

The Lord bless you and keep you;
  the Lord make His face shine upon you
  and be gracious to you;
  the Lord turn His face toward you
  and give you peace.

Numbers 6:24-26 (NIV)

A PRAYER FOR EVENING

Lord, receive our supplication for this
house, family and country. Protect the
innocent, restrain the greedy and the
treacherous, lead us out of our tribulation
into a quiet land. Look down upon ourselves and upon our absent dear ones. Help
us and them, prolong our days in peace and
honor. Give us health, food, bright weather
and light hearts. In what we meditate of
evil, frustrate our will; in what of good,
further our endeavors. Cause injuries to be
forgotten and benefits to be remembered.
Let us lie down without fear and awake and
arise with exultation. For His sake, in
whose words we now conclude.

—Robert Louis Stevenson

PRAYER

Lord, what a change within us one
    short hour
Spent in Thy presence will prevail to make!
What heavy burdens from our bosoms take,
What parched grounds refresh as
    with a shower!
We kneel and all around us seems to lower;
We rise, and all, the distant and the near,
Stands forth in sunny outline brave
    and clear;
We kneel, how weak! we rise,
    how full of power!
Why, therefore, should we do ourselves
    this wrong,
Or others, that we are not always strong,
That we are ever overborne with care,
That we should ever weak or heartless be,
Anxious or troubled, when with
    us is prayer,
And joy and strength and courage are with
    Thee!

—Richard C. Trench

WHAT IS PRAYER?

Prayer is the soul's sincere desire,
Uttered or unexpressed;
The motion of a hidden fire,
That trembles in the breast.

Prayer is the burden of a sigh;
The falling of a tear;
The upward glancing of an eye,
When none but God is near.

Prayer is the simplest form of speech
That infant lips can try;
Prayer, the sublimest strains that reach
The Majesty on high.

—James Montgomery

THE LARGER PRAYER

At first I prayed for Light:
Could I but see the way,
How gladly, swiftly would I walk
To everlasting day!

And next I prayed for Strength:
That I might tread the road
With firm, unfaltering feet, and win
The heaven's serene abode.

And then I asked for Faith:
Could I but trust my God,
I'd live enfolded in His peace,
Though foes were all abroad.

But now I pray for Love:
Deep love to God and man,
A living love that will not fail,
However dark His plan.

And Light and Strength and Faith
Are opening everywhere;
God only waited for me, till
I prayed the larger prayer.

—Edna D. Cheney

HE PRAYETH BEST

He prayeth best, who loveth best
All things both great and small;
For the dear God who loveth us,
He made and loveth all.

—Samuel Taylor Coleridge

WROUGHT BY PRAYER

More things are wrought by prayer
Than this world dreams of.
Wherefore, let thy voice
Rise like a fountain for me night and day.
For what are men better than sheep or goats
That nourish a blind life within the brain,
If, knowing God, they lift not hands of
    prayer
Both for themselves and those who call
    them friend?

—Alfred, Lord Tennyson

THE DIFFERENCE

I got up early one morning
And rushed right into the day;
I had so much to accomplish
That I didn't have time to pray.
Problems just tumbled about me,
And heavier came each task;
"Why doesn't God help me?"
   I wondered.
He answered, "You didn't ask."
I wanted to see joy and beauty,
But the day toiled on gray and bleak;
I wondered why God didn't show me.
He said, "But you didn't seek."
I tried to come into God's presence;
I used all my keys in the lock.
God gently and lovingly chided,
"My child, you didn't knock."
I woke up early this morning,
And paused before entering the day;
I had so much to accomplish
That I had to take time to pray.
              —Author Unknown

PEACE THROUGH PRAYER

Oft have I seen at some cathedral door
A laborer, pausing in the dust and heat,
Lay down his burden,
    and with reverent feet
Enter, and cross himself, and on the floor
Kneel to repeat his paternoster o'er;
Far off the noises of the world retreat;
The loud vociferations of the street
Become an undistinguishable roar.
So, as I enter here from day to day,
And leave my burden at this minster gate,
Kneeling in prayer,
    and not ashamed to pray,
The tumult of the time disconsolate
To inarticulate murmurs dies away,
While the eternal ages watch and wait.
          —*Henry Wadsworth Longfellow*

PRAYER

Be not afraid to pray—to pray is right.
Pray, if thou canst, with hope;
    but ever pray,
Though hope be weak,
    or sick with long delay;
Pray in the darkness, if there be no light.
Far is the time, remote from human sight,
When war and discord on the
    earth shall cease;
Yet every prayer for universal peace
Avails the blessed time to expedite.
Whate'er is good to wish,
    ask that of Heaven,
Though it be what thou canst not
    hope to see;
Pray to be perfect, though material leaven
Forbid the spirit so on earth to be:
But if for any wish thou darest not pray,
Then pray to God to cast that wish away.

—Hartley Coleridge

I SAID A PRAYER FOR YOU TODAY

I said a prayer for you today
And know God must have heard;
I felt the answer in my heart
Although He spoke not a word.

I didn't ask for wealth or fame
(I knew you wouldn't mind);
I asked for priceless treasures rare
Of a more lasting kind.

I prayed that He'd be near to you
At the start of each new day,
To grant you health and blessings fair,
And friends to share your way.

I asked for happiness for you
In all things great and small,
But that you'd know His loving care
I prayed the most of all.

—Author Unknown